MINNESOTA
VIKINGS

BY DAVE CAMPBELL

SportsZone

An Imprint of Abdo Publishing
abdopublishing.com

abdopublishing.com

Published by Abdo Publishing, a division of ABDO, PO Box 398166, Minneapolis, Minnesota 55439. Copyright © 2017 by Abdo Consulting Group, Inc. International copyrights reserved in all countries. No part of this book may be reproduced in any form without written permission from the publisher. SportsZone™ is a trademark and logo of Abdo Publishing.

Printed in the United States of America, North Mankato, Minnesota
042016
092016

Cover Photo: Ann Heisenfelt/AP Images
Interior Photos: Ann Heisenfelt/AP Images, 1, 26, 28-29; Tim Sharp/AP Images, 4-5; Carlos Osorio/AP Images, 6; Beth A. Keiser/AP Images, 7; Gene Herrick/AP Images, 8-9; Brian Horton/AP Images, 10-11; Owen C. Shaw/Icon Sportswire, 12-13; Bettmann/Corbis, 14; NFL Photos/AP Images, 15, 17; Eric Risberg/AP Images, 16; Duncan Livingston/AP Images, 18-19; Steve Castillo/AP Images, 20-21; David Durochik/AP Images, 22-23; Genevieve Ross/AP Images, 24-25; David Stluka/AP Images, 27

Editor: Patrick Donnelly
Series Designer: Nikki Farinella

Cataloging-in-Publication Data
Names: Campbell, Dave, author.
Title: Minnesota Vikings / by Dave Campbell.
Description: Minneapolis, MN : Abdo Publishing, [2017] | Series: NFL up close | Includes index.
Identifiers: LCCN 2015960443 | ISBN 9781680782233 (lib. bdg.) | ISBN 9781680776348 (ebook)
Subjects: LCSH: Minnesota Vikings (Football team)--History--Juvenile literature. | National Football League--Juvenile literature. | Football--Juvenile literature. | Professional sports--Juvenile literature. | Football teams--Minnesota--Juvenile literature.
Classification: DDC 796.332--dc23
LC record available at http://lccn.loc.gov/2015960443

TABLE OF CONTENTS

GREAT IN '98 4

VIKINGS SET SAIL 8

GRANT AND GLORY 12

LATE 1980s SURGE 16

GREEN LEADS THE WAY 20

FROM ADRIAN TO ZIMMER 24

Timeline 30
Glossary 31
Index / About the Author 32

GREAT IN '98

In 1998, the Minnesota Vikings traveled to Green Bay, Wisconsin, to face their biggest rivals, the Packers. Rookie wide receiver Randy Moss was playing in his first Monday Night Football game. He made a good first impression.

Moss and quarterback Randall Cunningham made it look easy. Cunningham lofted the ball high and deep. Moss outjumped everybody to make the catch. Moss finished the game with five receptions for 190 yards and two touchdowns. The Vikings rolled to a 37-24 victory.

FAST FACT

Fueled by wide receivers Randy Moss, Cris Carter, and Jake Reed, the Vikings scored 556 points in 1998. That National Football League (NFL) record stood for nine years.

Randy Moss made it look easy as a rookie with the Minnesota Vikings in 1998.

Beating the Packers in Green Bay was just one of many highlights in 1998. The Vikings went 15-1, setting a team record for victories. But the best season in team history had a rough finish.

The Vikings were one win away from the Super Bowl. They led the Atlanta Falcons 27-20 late in the game. Kicker Gary Anderson lined up for a 38-yard field goal. He had made 44 field goals in a row. But he missed that one wide left. The Falcons scored the tying touchdown. Then they beat the Vikings in overtime.

Randall Cunningham had a career year for the Vikings in 1998.

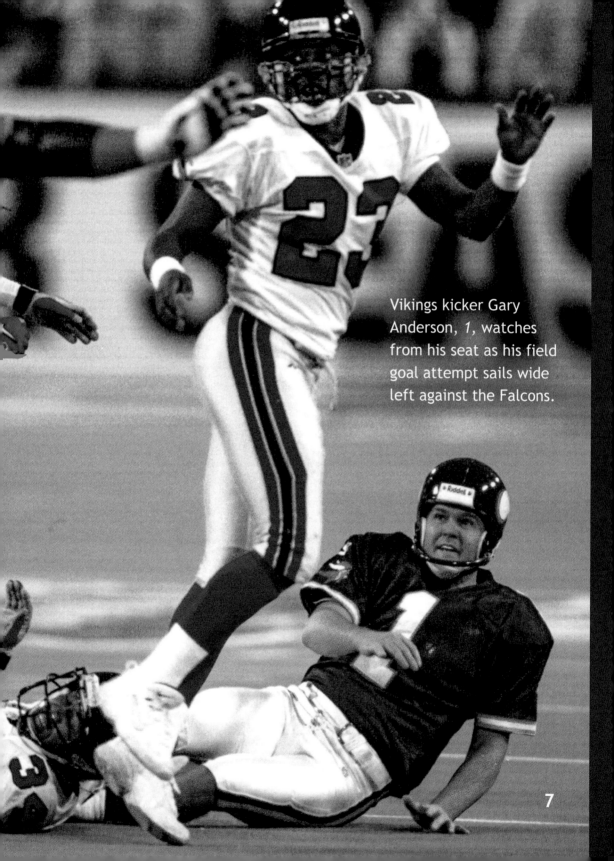

Vikings kicker Gary Anderson, *1*, watches from his seat as his field goal attempt sails wide left against the Falcons.

Running back Hugh McElhenny shows that Vikings like all types of boats as he paddles a canoe on Lake Bemidji, near the site of the team's first training camp in 1961.

8

VIKINGS SET SAIL

The NFL granted Minnesota a new team for the 1961 season. General manager Bert Rose recommended the name Vikings. These warriors once roamed the waters of northern Europe. They were aggressive and fierce. Vikings are associated with Norway. Many Minnesotans trace their roots back to that country.

FAST FACT

Minnesota's first coach was Norm Van Brocklin. He was the league's Most Valuable Player (MVP) in 1960 as quarterback of the NFL champion Philadelphia Eagles.

Vikings quarterback Fran Tarkenton was best known for his ability to escape the pass rush and find a receiver downfield.

FAST FACT

The Vikings have played in the same division as the Chicago Bears, Detroit Lions, and Green Bay Packers since 1961.

It took the Vikings four years to post a winning record and eight years to make the playoffs. Their first game, though, was a smashing success. Rookie quarterback Fran Tarkenton totaled five touchdowns as the Vikings beat the Chicago Bears 37-13.

Bud Grant coached Minnesota to four Super Bowls in his 18 seasons with the Vikings.

GRANT AND GLORY

The Vikings hired Bud Grant to coach the team in 1967. Grant had been a star athlete at the University of Minnesota. He won a championship playing for the Minneapolis Lakers of the National Basketball Association (NBA). And he had a long, successful career playing and coaching football in Canada.

Under Grant's stern leadership, the Vikings reached their first Super Bowl two seasons later. They were the first modern expansion team to make it that far. Minnesota lost to the Kansas City Chiefs, but it was the start of a golden era for the Vikings.

FAST FACT

Bud Grant is the only person to have played in the NFL and the NBA.

The Vikings reached the Super Bowl four times in eight seasons (1969 to 1976). They lost all four Super Bowls, but it was not for a lack of talent or toughness. The heart of those teams was the defensive line. Carl Eller, Gary Larsen, Jim Marshall, and Alan Page played together from 1967 to 1974. They terrorized quarterbacks and stuffed running backs at the line. They were called "The Purple People Eaters."

Six players from the 1970s Vikings teams wound up in the Pro Football Hall of Fame. Page, Eller, and safety Paul Krause represented the defense. They were joined by quarterback Fran Tarkenton, center Mick Tingelhoff, and tackle Ron Yary.

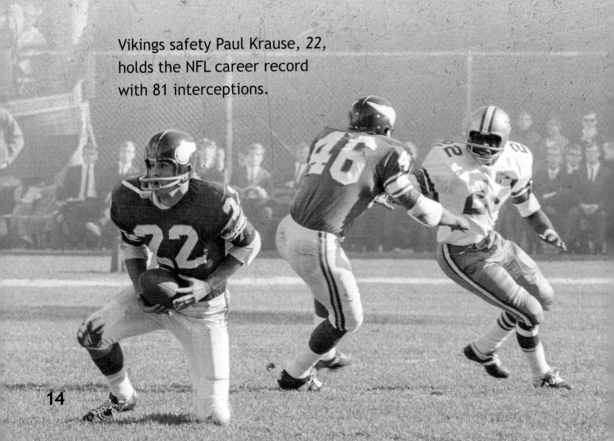

Vikings safety Paul Krause, 22, holds the NFL career record with 81 interceptions.

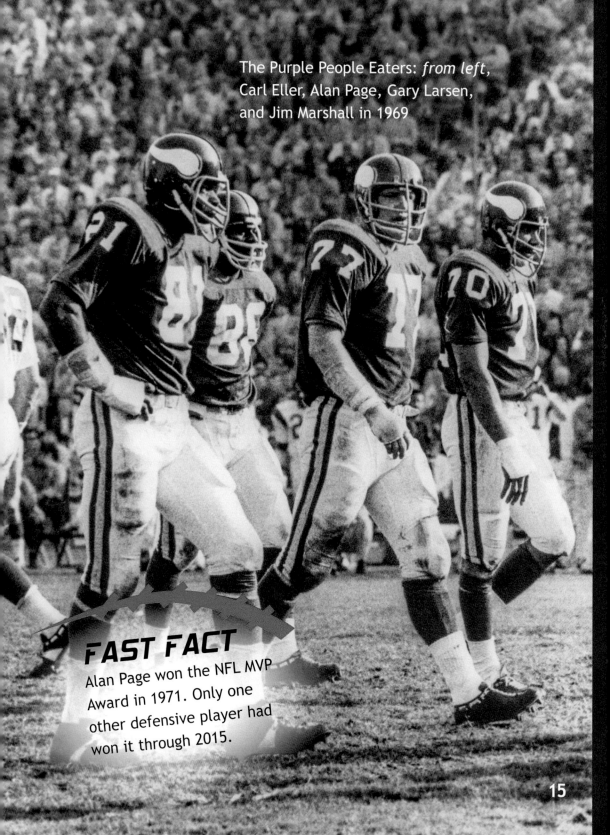

The Purple People Eaters: *from left,* Carl Eller, Alan Page, Gary Larsen, and Jim Marshall in 1969

FAST FACT

Alan Page won the NFL MVP Award in 1971. Only one other defensive player had won it through 2015.

LATE 1980s SURGE

Bud Grant retired after the 1985 season. New coach Jerry Burns led the team to the playoffs three straight years starting in 1987. That first season, the Vikings barely made the playoffs. But as heavy underdogs, they blew out the New Orleans Saints and San Francisco 49ers on the road.

They were within one game of the Super Bowl. Minnesota trailed Washington 17-10 with just under a minute left. On fourth down, a pass slipped through Vikings running back Darrin Nelson's hands at the goal line. Minnesota had come up short again.

Anthony Carter had 10 catches for 227 yards as the Vikings shocked the San Francisco 49ers 36-24 in the 1987 NFL playoffs.

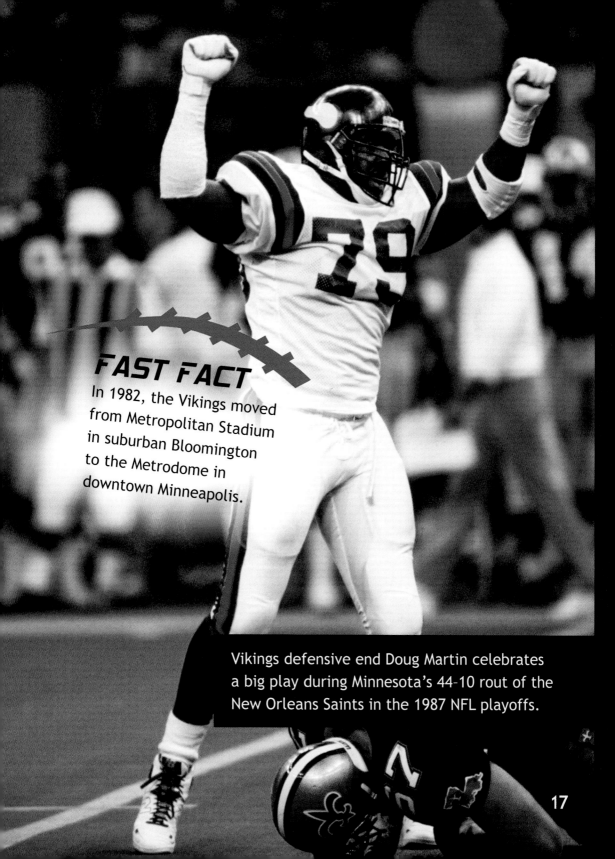

Vikings defensive end Doug Martin celebrates a big play during Minnesota's 44-10 rout of the New Orleans Saints in the 1987 NFL playoffs.

17

In 1989, the Vikings thought they were one player away from having a championship team. They wanted a standout running back, and the Dallas Cowboys wanted to trade former Heisman Trophy winner Herschel Walker. Minnesota sent five players and eight future draft picks to Dallas in exchange for Walker.

The Vikings did make the playoffs that year, but they lost in the first round. Walker was a major disappointment and only played two more years for the Vikings. Meanwhile, the Cowboys won three Super Bowls in the early 1990s. They used the draft picks they got from the Vikings to acquire many of their best players.

FAST FACT

Randall McDaniel anchored Minnesota's offensive line from 1988 through 1999. The Hall of Fame left guard was a first-team All-Pro seven times in his 11 years with the Vikings.

Herschel Walker, *34*, has a rare big gain for the Vikings against the Seattle Seahawks in 1990.

GREEN LEADS THE WAY

In 1992, Dennis Green took over as the Vikings' new coach. In his first year, the team finished 11-5 and won its division. That was the start of another great stretch of football in Minnesota.

The Vikings relied on the loud Metrodome crowds to give them an advantage. They put up big offensive numbers. And they reached the playoffs eight times in Green's first nine seasons.

FAST FACT

The Vikings signed Randall Cunningham out of retirement in 1997. He had spent the previous year working at his marble and granite business in Las Vegas, Nevada.

Dennis Green had a successful run as the Vikings' coach in the 1990s.

After the dramatic 1998 playoff loss to the Atlanta Falcons, the Vikings were back in the conference title game two years later. They were on the road but favored to beat the New York Giants. Instead, they lost 41–0.

Green left Minnesota late in the 2001 season. His teams went 97–62 in the regular season, but they won just four of 12 playoff games.

Hall of Fame wide receiver Cris Carter had back-to-back 122-catch seasons for the Vikings in 1994 and 1995.

Adrian Peterson, 28, recovered from a devastating knee injury to win the NFL rushing title in 2012.

FROM ADRIAN TO ZIMMER

The Vikings drafted running back Adrian Peterson with their first-round pick in 2007. He put the team's offense on his back immediately. Peterson racked up an NFL-record 296 yards rushing in one game as a rookie. He won the NFL rushing title the next year with 1,760 yards.

But his most impressive feat was in 2012. Peterson suffered a severe knee injury in December 2011. He came back the next season determined to prove the surgery would not slow him down. He was better than ever. Peterson rushed for 2,097 yards, just nine short of the league's single-season record. He carried the Vikings to a surprise playoff berth and was named the NFL MVP.

Peterson was a superstar. But the Vikings did not often have such a star to line up at quarterback in the early 2000s. Daunte Culpepper had five solid years under center in Minnesota, but a serious knee injury in 2005 shortened his career. Soon, the Vikings turned to an old rival to put them back in the championship hunt.

Brett Favre was a villain to Minnesota fans over 16 seasons as the Green Bay Packers' quarterback. In 2009, Favre put on purple and at age 40 had the best year of his career. He helped Minnesota beat the Packers twice. The Vikings reached the conference title game again, but they suffered another painful overtime loss. This time it was on the road against the New Orleans Saints.

The Vikings' home field was unavailable when the Metrodome roof collapsed in a snowstorm in 2010.

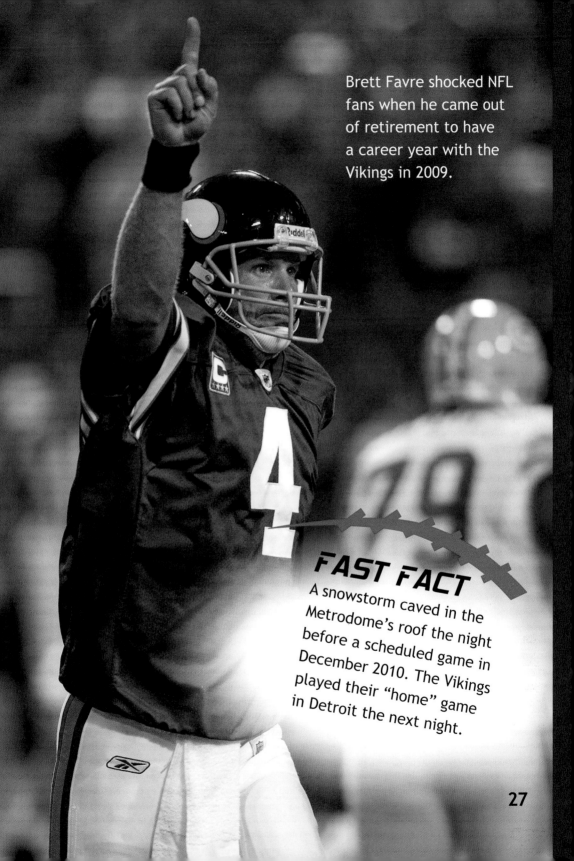

Brett Favre shocked NFL fans when he came out of retirement to have a career year with the Vikings in 2009.

FAST FACT

A snowstorm caved in the Metrodome's roof the night before a scheduled game in December 2010. The Vikings played their "home" game in Detroit the next night.

FAST FACT

The Vikings played outdoors at the University of Minnesota for two years while their new stadium was being built.

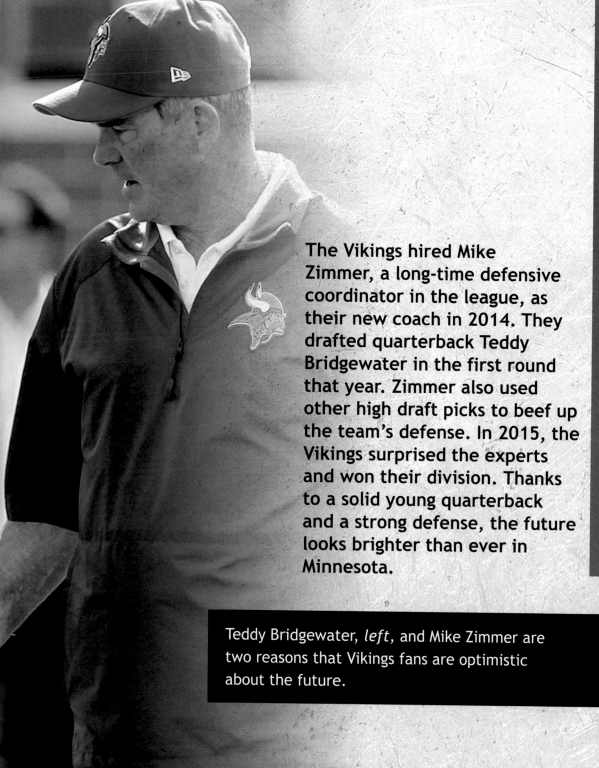

The Vikings hired Mike Zimmer, a long-time defensive coordinator in the league, as their new coach in 2014. They drafted quarterback Teddy Bridgewater in the first round that year. Zimmer also used other high draft picks to beef up the team's defense. In 2015, the Vikings surprised the experts and won their division. Thanks to a solid young quarterback and a strong defense, the future looks brighter than ever in Minnesota.

Teddy Bridgewater, *left*, and Mike Zimmer are two reasons that Vikings fans are optimistic about the future.

TIMELINE

1961

The Vikings play their first regular-season game on September 17. Rookie quarterback Fran Tarkenton sparks a 37-13 victory over the Chicago Bears.

1970

The Vikings play in their first Super Bowl, losing 23-7 to the Kansas City Chiefs on January 11.

1972

Quarterback Fran Tarkenton returns to Minnesota. He had played the previous five years with the New York Giants.

1977

On January 9, the Vikings lose their fourth Super Bowl, falling 32-14 to the Oakland Raiders.

1981

The Vikings play their final game at Metropolitan Stadium, losing 10-6 to Kansas City on December 20. They move into the Metrodome the next season.

1998

The Vikings go 15-1 and set an NFL record for points scored in a season.

2013

The Vikings play their final game at the Metrodome, beating the Detroit Lions 14-13 on December 29.

2016

On January 10, the Vikings lose a playoff game to the Seattle Seahawks 10-9 in the coldest game in team history. The temperature at kickoff was minus-6 degrees Fahrenheit (-21°C).

GLOSSARY

ALL-PRO
A player voted as the best in the NFL at his position in a season.

COORDINATOR
An assistant coach who is in charge of a team's offense or defense.

DIVISION
A group of teams that help form a league.

EXPANSION
When a league grows by adding new teams.

FIELD GOAL
A kick worth three points if it travels through the goal posts.

GOAL LINE
The edge of the end zone that a player must cross with the ball to score a touchdown.

OVERTIME
An extra period or periods played in the event of a tie.

ROOKIE
A first-year player.

UNDERDOG
The person or team that is not expected to win.

INDEX

Anderson, Gary, 6, 7

Bridgewater, Teddy, 29

Burns, Jerry, 16

Carter, Anthony, 16
Carter, Cris, 4, 22
Culpepper, Daunte, 26
Cunningham, Randall, 4, 6, 20

Eller, Carl, 14, 15

Favre, Brett, 26, 27

Grant, Bud, 12, 13, 16
Green, Dennis, 20, 21, 22

Krause, Paul, 14

Larsen, Gary, 14, 15

Marshall, Jim, 14, 15
Martin, Doug, 17
McDaniel, Randall, 18
McElhenny, Hugh, 8
Moss, Randy, 4, 5

Nelson, Darrin, 16

Page, Alan, 14, 15
Peterson, Adrian, 24, 25-26

Reed, Jake, 4
Rose, Bert, 9

Tarkenton, Fran, 10, 11, 14
Tingelhoff, Mick, 14

Van Brocklin, Norm, 9

Walker, Herschel, 18, 19

Yary, Ron, 14

Zimmer, Mike, 29

ABOUT THE AUTHOR

Dave Campbell has reported and written about the Vikings for The Associated Press since 2001 and has followed them since the mid-1980s. He lives in Minneapolis with his wife and his son.